Don't Say I Passed Away

Poetry of Life, Death, Love and Loss

By Louisa C. Sciolla

Dedication

For all of my loves, lovers, teachers and friends
You know who you are!!!

Defenseless

Sometimes
I still get that feeling
Like a boulder
On a hummingbird
On my heart
Both heavy and frantic
A slow-moving panic

What once left me breathless
Has left me defenseless
When these memories
Come calling
I almost can't breathe

Lovely Little Lie

My strength lies almost entirely
In my vulnerability
If you ask me how I am
If you are a person I trust
Love or even like
I'm going to tell the truth
In all honesty
Lately it hasn't been so good
If you want me to tell a lovely little lie
Don't ask
Just smile and keep on walking by
Imagine I said something light and pleasant
I will imagine that you see the strength
In my beautiful vulnerability
I will imagine that you understand
That I can be both heartbroken by life and
Happy to be on this amazing trip
Happy to be me
Knowing that living in truth has set me free

In Lieu of You

At night
In lieu of you
I wish to be alone
Someday possibly
I'll heal these cracks
I'll give love more try

It's late and quiet
This peace reminds me
Saturdays long past
I was your home
I still find myself
Waiting
Like a passenger
Forever on standby

I planned to love again and soon
To be loved back
Passionately and boundlessly
Sharing my soul
With someone who wanted all of me
Somehow my plans have gone awry

Beautiful Demise

So much unexpected joy
Led to loss I can't describe
My most beautiful demise
Leaving me
With love in the tears streaming
From your eyes
Already missing me
Yet saying your goodbyes

All of Me

Enthralled
By his beautiful eyes
Green like spring
Deep like the sea

The most beautiful thing
About those eyes
Without judgement or criticism
They saw all of me

Although
I may not look into them
Ever again
In their thrall
I'll always be

Rich in Love

Looking at his face
There was no greater opulence
I was rich in love
In adoration
The splendor of getting lost
In the beauty of the beloved
Is greater than all the riches of the earth
No gold or jewels
Could adorn me
Like my heart inflamed
No silken fabric could cover my body
Like love untamed

A Dare

You asked if I was afraid to
Be with someone so young
You asked as if it was a dare
I have to admit love
I didn't see the danger
I didn't know how much I'd come to care

I was so fascinated by our attraction
Enamored with your beauty
In my infatuation
I didn't stop to ponder
How much you'd still have to wander
To find yourself

I was just so happy that I found you
(or you'd found me, in reality)
I didn't stop to think
How I would feel when you disappeared
In the end
You were everything I didn't know to fear

Broken Meter

I don't think that
Anyone
Has ever loved me
With the intensity
As actively
As I love

Either my meter
Is broken or
I am more powerful
Than most
Either way
In Love
I have mostly been alone

Celestial Realm

Sun hides
Behind dark
Clouds
Who can blame her
She rarely sees her love
Oh, but the moon meets the sun
More than I'll ever meet with you
Still, I'm grateful to share a galaxy
Though I'd love to share a smaller one
A Celestial realm built for just two

Once Real

There are times that
My imagination
Is more real than
My reality
Only in my imagination
Are you ever here
My once real lover
Has become my dream lover
In dreams you always
Have a place with me

Mirror, Mirror

I miss my favorite mirror
It was so true
Reflecting the best and
Worst of me
Through you

Seeing myself so clearly
Was sometimes painful
I saw my beauty in a new light too

I will be forever grateful
For the kindness
In those eyes
For all of you

Crashing

Crashing
Burning
Stomach churning
Sick to death
This drawn out yearning
Is surprisingly extant
Something missing

Grateful?

Every day is a gift
Unique from the others
I should be so grateful
I almost lost them all
Still

There are days
That celebrating this life
Is too exhausting
Days I wonder why
I lived at all

There is no defining moment
That life becomes pure magic
Even miracles leave us
Right where we left off

Growth is always painful
Life is always hard
Always precious
Just living, just breathing is enough

Not Fair

I come home from every date
Feeling that it's
Not going to happen
Not ever

The thing I wanted
You wanted to avoid
Yet you found it (somewhere else)
When all I could do
Was think of you

You found what I wanted
What you didn't
With someone else
I found that you are
One of the loves of my life

I want to scream like a child
IT'S NOT FAIR

But love never is

Strange

I don't fit in your box
My shapes are too strange
My edges too raw
I can't fit in your box
However
If you want to come out
I'll show you my
Strangely shaped soul
Tell you
The many reasons
Why I must remain strange
To remain whole
Maybe then you'll finally see
That you don't really fit
Just like me

Shallow

I would rather
A thousand deaths
Of drowning
My lungs full of deep truth
Bursting with reality
Than one day in the shallow end
Faking a pretty smile
So that everybody likes me

Imaginary Spring

Fresh thoughts
Spring up like
Bright blooms
As though you and I
Could
Like spring
Renew
Me reborn
New born you
Grass green eyes meet
Pink petal lips
Kissing sweet
Happy tears
Water us like rain
We grow
We flower
We love again

Naked

Naked
I want to be
Honest and raw
Without fear of loss
The goddess
And the fucking mess
Share everything
And nothing less
I want to be
Completely
Naked

Scarred

Cancer
Left me
Scarred for life
With an ability
To sit
With pain and fear
With self-love
Even during drastic change
With a fervent
Desire to live
With a constant
Desire to love
With a deep and enduring
Desire to give

Glittering Star

The dream
I never want to wake from
The alternate reality
Where I want to live and die
The film
I laugh and cry to
In deepest night
You
My love
The glittering Star
That comes to me in sleep
You are my dream
You are the light

Isn't It Unromantic

I don't know how to live
In this world that we have
So recklessly
Created
The things I want
Feel hopelessly
Dated
The lack of romance
Slowly killing me
Vapid words
(good vibes only)
Strangely chilling to me
More connectivity than ever
Yet rampant loneliness
Is a symptom
Of our digital disease
I'm not sure I'd choose to live
In this world
But my being out of time
Seems to be fated

We All Bleed

The pain of
Heartache
May just be
One of the strongest
Ties
That binds us all
Together
I hold all of your
Lost pieces
In my most sacred space
In the humanity
We find in our
Collective losses
I feel less alone

Burning

I cozied up
Next to the warmth
Held my frozen hands out
Sighed contentedly as they thawed
In the blissful heat
Of love
The blaze of life
We search for
In the cold of night
Happy to finally be
In the presence of sacred fire
I never noticed
That I began to burn
I wouldn't have
Couldn't have
Walked away
From the spark that drew me
Anyway

For Now

I think for now
I will love
The sky
My father
The ocean
The sunset
My mother
The moon
My two brothers
All creatures
Large and small
Constellations
Possibilities
Myself
And you, of course still you

Faerie

I was made for
Meadow dancing
Drinking from
The honeysuckle cup
Whispering secret dreams
Into the ears of sleeping beauties
Lighting up the night sky
With my luminous wings
In my heart
I am a faerie
A worshipper of nature
A midnight reveler
In my soul
Exists
A magical
Whimsical being

Aphrodite

Sometimes I catch myself
Praying to Gods I don't believe in
That heartbreak
Has not broken me
I am too romantic
Too be so cynical
I have far too much to give
To always be alone
Sometimes I catch myself praying
To the deities inside of me
For a blessing I sometimes think
Impossible
That my heart will find a home

Invisible

I sit waiting
For a reason
Any reason
To step out
Into the light
I have grown
Too accustomed
To the shadows
Of the night
I have become
An expert at hiding
In plain site

Maybe I really do
Just want to rest here
A bit longer
On my own

Pearl In The Lotus

Those pieces of my heart
The ones I left with you
Please keep them
Like lost treasure
The pearl in the lotus
An engagement ring lost
Settled in the bottom of a lake
I won't miss them
As I still sometimes miss you
They have regenerated
Grown back stronger
My patchwork heart
Stitched together with
Self-love and sweet memories
Phantom kisses and hard-won peace

Flowering

Flowers grow out of my ribcage
Roots grow deep into my lungs
My heart has grown a garden
From seeds left behind
That in my sadness
I had ungratefully
Mistaken for crumbs

Malnourished

You feed her doubt
More than you nourish her heart
And wonder why
She seems so
Anxious and insecure
About you
About love

Your Corner

No reason for me
To still be here
Doggedly
In your corner
I just don't know
Where else to go
I live like a ghost
Haunting
Quietly wanting
To come back to life
In this corner
I should not still be here
But leaving has a permanency
A final destitution of loss
That I can't bear

Quietly

This doesn't hurt
Like it used to
It's more a dull
Intermittent ache
The waves get further apart
Less powerful
Far less likely
To wash me away
While continuing
Daily
To quietly break

We're All Gonna Die

Guess what?
You're going to die
As am I
Let's live life accordingly
Someday we won't be here
All mistakes forgotten
Failures dust in the wind
But the love
The love you give
Will echo for eternity
Instead of holding on to hate
We can forgive
And give
And give

Why not?
We're going to die

Jewel Box Sky

When I die
I hope not soon
Like a new star
In a velvet jewel box sky
I will shine bright
Eternal
Because I love
Because I am loved
Because I am love

Attachment Vs Freedom

Set them free
So romantic
Such a lovely thought
A Dalai Deepak Disney thought
But love can feel like life and death
Caught up in the drama
It's hard to catch your breath
To calm the fuck down
When faced with loss
Set them free
I wish that I could always be
So gracefully evolved
It's not possible
When every square inch
Of my loving heart
Is intimately
Entangled and involved

Stripped

Stripped naked
You see the inner workings
Of my soul
I bare myself
To anyone who will read me
In hopes
That shedding
The darkest
Pieces of myself
Dripping these thoughts on paper
As though I were losing blood
Will help me to find my way back
To my own light
And make me whole

Strength

In bed
Late
High on oxy
Wondering what these scars
Will look like someday
Has it spread?
Is this what will kill me?
Break my family's collective heart?
So many questions
No finite answers
Just hope
And belief in my own
Hard earned strength

My Universe

My universe is so different now
My nebula have faded
My brightest stars
Become black holes
Living through
My own personal big bang
Has spawned both growth
And destruction
Leaving me with more stardust
From which to form
New galaxies
With great loss
Comes the power to recreate

Too late

I have said
The wrong thing
The wrong way
Too many times to count
My heart is big
Unfortunately
Occasionally
My mouth is bigger
Is it too late to make atonement?
Have my verbal transgressions
Caused too much damage?
Do I make amends
Or just take the lesson?
I have too much regret
For a person
With such good intentions

Impermanent

I have studied enough philosophy
To know that
Impermanence is the only constant
The only thing to depend on
Why then
Do I also know
That you are indelibly inked
Into my soul
Tattooed in my most sacred spaces
With ink that never fades
This knowledge of you
Will only die when I do
I guess this love
Is impermanent after all

Subtle Madness

I have a soft spot
A place in my heart
For rabble rousers
Creative iconoclasts
Those who feel deeply
Painters
Writers
Music makers
Anyone who insists
On making life into art
Makes me feel at home
With my own
Subtle madness
That is my desire
To live passionately

Wild Love

Would that I could
Put it in a box
Tied up with
A red satin ribbon
Bury it under
A weeping willow
Near a lazy river
To be dug up
Admired at a much
Later date
Its potency watered
Down by time and age
Regrettably
Wild love
Creates equally wild heartache
Always to remain
Beautifully
Dangerously
Uncontained

The Rain

Drops from heaven
Pelt my face
Oceans wind blows my hair
Love for life
Lifts my spirits
Fills my primitive
Mermaid soul
For this hour
In the presence
Of my mother
The sea
I feel as close to whole
The most me
I'll ever be

Mine

I have shared parts of me
Opened to a lucky few
Given until it seemed
There was no more to give
But in the end
I am mine
All mine
The pieces I give
Are just clones
I stay whole
I could give you
The moon and stars
While still staying me
I could let you become
A part of me
And still my love
I would still
Stay mine

Chemistry

Synapses in my neocortex
Sparkle and sing
At the mere thought of you
You have altered
My brain chemistry
Permanently
Leaving me no choice
But to wait
For someone
Who understands
My specific
Neurobiology
A man of science
A dealer of pure
Uncut love
Who will lure me in
With that first hit
A new addiction
A potent new compound
That makes me high
In a way
That doesn't make me
Cry

Shards

There are shards of me
In all your pockets
You jingle them
Like keys
Do you ever take them out
To see them sparkle
In the moonlight?
Or maybe just to let them breathe?
There are shards of me
In all your pockets
You can ignore them
But they will always be

Fear

Fear is insidious
It creeps silently
Into everyday life
Stopping us from enjoying
Simple pleasures
A walk in the moonlight
Smiling at strangers
Or wearing that dress
That makes you feel pretty
Fear is the fiend's way
Of ending our life as we know it
Killing our freedom
Even as we still breathe

Mara (I See You)

Separateness is an illusion
While it is not necessary
To invite everyone you meet
Into your life
It is not wise to trust blindly
It is useful to remember
That discernment is necessary
But judgement is not
We need to remember
That we are inseparable
From one another
There is no real difference
It is the same red
That flows when we bleed

Mixed Feelings

Feelings are not mutually exclusive
Love
Anger
Disappointment
And Regret
Can all be present in one place
Just to name a few
Adoration and attrition
Independence and deep desire for oneness
Are often partners too
The building of a safe container
For this potent vortex of emotions
Is more reasonable a goal
Than any attempt
To forget you
Feelings are not mutually exclusive
I'm learning how to hold them all
While trying to build my life anew

Magic

In search of simple pleasures
We stumbled on
Each other's magic
Enchanted by both dark and light
We shone brighter
Threw longer shadows
Every hour spent together
Every sacred night
You have stopped believing
Although it's still alight
Still there in our hearts depths
Hidden safely
Out of sight

Anniversary

The day my life changed
You were there
Not as a lover
But as someone who cared
Witnessing my pain and fear
You were my shining knight
It was somehow easier with you near
On that terrifying day
I felt something close to happy
As crazy as it sounds
Mixing morphine and lost love
Creates a very heady drug
Thank you for that day
Your presence meant more
Than words could ever say
Fuck you for the way
Knowing that my life
Hung in the balance
Was irrevocably changed
With no goodbye
You disappeared

Keep shining

If someone should tell you
To dim your light
Burn ever brighter
For yourself
Take your starlight from their sight
Keep shining
For those who love your light
And those who don't
Leave them in the dark

Morning Moon

I woke up just before dawn
To see her burning bright
Feeling that she
Had caressed
And tormented me
All through the night
Reminding me
Of every high and low
All the love
All the loss
Every kiss she'd witnessed
Every sleepless night
Alone

Emancipated

Pathologically emancipated
From reality
My traumas separate me
From the mundane
The everyday
Giving me the power
To decide
What's important
What's ok
The rules of society
No longer apply to me
I've been through far too much
To just obey

Depth

They wear lighter colors
Say sweeter things
Have more "friends"
Attend more things
With smiles
That look freshly clipped
From beauty magazines
Such a pretty picture
If you don't look too closely
You won't have to
See the vital thing that's missing
The thing that makes life worth living
I think they call it depth

Fine Thanks

I woke to the sound
Of a homeless man screaming
In made up languages
That sounded like I was still dreaming
It suddenly hit me
Maybe we are crazy
Maybe he us sane
We drag around
Our histories and heartbreaks
Sometimes coping well
Happy
Others internally bleeding
Smiling politely
Saying nothing
Endlessly repeating
"Fine thanks, how are you?"

Shadow Self

When I said my sun had gone
My shadow started to shrink
She doesn't understand metaphors
Because she doesn't actually think
When she heard my moon had gone
My shadow tried to hide
She cried to herself quietly
Every time we went outside
I tried to make her understand
That we would be ok
But she ran into a closet
And locked herself away

Almost Loved

How I loved
Almost being
Loved by you
It was enough
Just barely
To almost
Get us through
I gave you my everything
Lover
It was far too much and also
Too little for you

High

Is there really
A low
To balance
Every high
A long fall
To plummet to
Every time you fly
This would explain love perfectly
Those highs
They draw me in
Every damn time
Wanna get high?

I Am

I am dirty clean
Sweet and mean
You saw it all
You embraced it
This gift
Will be forever mine
Acceptance from a love
Whose love was not blind

Lost

The day I looked
Into your eyes
And the words
"You're beautiful"
Escaped my lips
Was my point
Of no return
It's ok love
I don't want
The parts me I gave
Returned
Except maybe
My fears
My thoughtless words
Or anything
That hurt you
Except maybe

My heart

Malignant

I didn't die
The chances
Of recurrence
Are low enough
To bet on
But it was malignant
Fast growing
Wanting me
I am grateful
For my life
Of course
But this
Dance with death
Is a lot to live with
I don't want to die
Young or painfully
I don't want to die

That way

Love Is

It is so many things
Passionate nights
Respectful fights
Being excited
Even when it's no longer new
Seeing everything you ever hoped for
In your beloved's eyes
Feeling heartbreak when he cries
Saying I'd do anything for you
Knowing that it is completely true
Most importantly
It's staying
When things get rough
Because there is no choice
He's the only one for you

Apology

Professing feelings of guilt
Is not the same
As a heartfelt apology
It's how you feel about you
Not something you give to me
I have no desire for revenge
No need for retribution
A simple
I'm sorry I wasn't there
Would have been enough
But love
I know
That apologizing
Is no easy thing
Much easier to focus
On the ways that I've wronged you

My Clique

Unable to shape myself
Into a more pleasing object
For the masses
I prefer time alone
Or time spent with kindred souls
The only clique I've ever joined
Is made up of
My thoughts
My loves
My many dreams
A million grains of sand
A forest full of trees
Multitudes that allow
For space
In which
My mind and soul can roam free

On Gun Violence
An American Epidemic

The parents
The grandparents
The friends
The neighbors
The tragic loss of
So much potential
Another community
Left in trauma
A country saddened
Shocked and outraged
Again
While not a fucking thing changes
Our country is a monster
That breeds monsters
While the politicians pander
To the hand that feeds them
While the other hand kills children
With no remorse

Post Script
(I am slowly seeing and hoping for change)

Wants

I want
Someone who looks at me
Like I look at the moon
Who loves me
With the passion that I feel for the sunset
Who will swim in me
Like I do the ocean
Someone to warm me
Like the early summer sun

Spring

Early spring rain
Awakens nature
Like a playful splash
Between children in a pool
Renewal promised
As the season changes
Look outside
Beauty reigns

Never the Same

I loved him madly
Like thunder and lightning
Passionate and beautiful
Occasionally frightening
Bringing with it
Driving rain

I now love him dearly
Like sunshine and a soft breeze
And the occasional violent passion
Of a sudden summer squall

Someday I'll love him softly
Like starlight
On a night lit only
By a tiny a sliver of moon
Floating on the horizon
Never showing its face

When love is real
Love remains
Constantly changing
Always present
Never the same

Still Sorry

I can't seem to let it go
I am still sorry
And I cannot let you know
I am so sorry
That I let you down
With my tendency
To share my vulnerability
With people
That I trust
Because they've
Shared their own with me
I am so sorry
That my humanity
Was so painful
For you to see
That you couldn't stick around
When I needed you
You couldn't just be there for me

Marama

I love how lovers
Commune with the moon
When his ears
Became deaf to me
I told her all my sorrows
She heard every word
When I feel alone
La Luna always listens lovingly
I tell her things
I never got a chance to say to you
When I feel hopeless
I speak to her
And whether full
Or the tiny sliver when she's new
When my soul feels shattered
Marama sees me through

(Marama is the Maori word for moon)

Rise Above

I create
Because
I am a daughter of creation
I love so well
Because
I am born of love
I am afraid
But fear is not what
I am made of
It is something
That I have to rise above

Always

My skin will always
Remember your touch
My lips
Have recorded your kiss
I will always remember
The pain and the pleasure
Love surrendering to lust
The sweetness of surrender
Only possible
When my heart feels total trust
From the first to last kiss
A short
But forever cherished
Time of bliss

Queendom

Queen of my own
Little universe
I sit in contemplation on my
Astral throne
Of stars, jewels and flowers
Lost in daydreams of
A future
When the world
Becomes as peaceful
As my tiny little queendom
When love will replace
Base currency
When we finally learn
That we must take care of our own

Looking Glass

Dear you
Yes you
On the other side
Of my overused
Looking glass
I may look too often
With a critical eye
But I promise
That I love you
Just the way you are
Life hurts sometimes
Love hurts often
But I will always
No matter what we go through
I will always
Always
Come back to you

I fell

Sometimes
It still hits me
Right in the gut
Like a knife or a bullet
I fell in love
Blindly
Beautifully
Utterly
In love
It's been gone
For so long
While remaining
Right here
A wraith
My hands can't touch
But pass right through
My lips can't kiss
The pain feels new
You stayed on your feet
I fell to my knees
Falling completely
In love with you

Emergency

The happiest I've been
In recent memory
The emergency room
Shivering with pain
Doctors discovering
An almost certain case of cancer
And yet I felt high and happy
In a terrible situation
Morphine and you
Should be an illegal combination

Trick of The Light

From my doorway
I see our ghosts
In my bed
It's strange
I didn't even know
We were dead
I still see us sometimes
Looking very alive
It must be a trick of the light

Both sides

To be both
A realist and
A romantic
Is to know
Damn well
It won't work
And
To try
Entirely too hard
Just in case

No Future

Although
I didn't dare
Picture
A picture perfect
Future
I did
Get so far in
That
For the life of me
I couldn't imagine
The end

Finite

My heart is filled
With stars
Solar systems
Galaxies
Freely through
A celestial plain
Big enough for two
This infinity
I hold in
My most sacred space
Is not so well suited
To the finite nature
Of romantic love

The Sensitive

The sensitive
The beautiful
Of heart and mind
Are needed here
In this ugly time
We cannot afford
The loss of
One more lovely soul
Please remember
When it gets bad
When you feel too alone
That not one of us
Consistently feels whole

To Live

Love Passionately
Love with abandon
With all of your heart
But don't give it away
If it doesn't feel
Like a fair exchange
You may need it someday
To pump your life's blood
Through your newly wounded body
To live
To love again

Love Unleashes

I can be
The best of friends
A safe port to rest
Wild with loss
The most sensual seductress
Feral animal
The most natural nurturer
A depressive catatonic
Childlike in my joy
Angry force of nature
Or a loving mother earth

It depends on the moons phase
It depends on how you love me

Hard Truth

It's true
No matter what you do
How much you try to hide
The people you love
Will at some point see you
At your ugliest
Out of control
Raging and vulnerable

It is not always true
That they will still love you whole
They may step out
Before you give your encore

Debt

Whatever I did
Way back when
Must have been
Truly deplorable
In my last life
I clearly did something
Horrible
I am ready to move on
From all the pain
That I have met
Tell me
Bodhisattva
Have I paid my debt yet?

Magic and Medicine

Sometimes
I forget
And then I undress
My scars
Stare back at me
Lovingly
Magic and medicine
Conspired to keep me alive
Some say miraculous
I say
Perhaps a mixed blessing

Abandonment

My greatest fear
Has always been
Somewhat rationally
Abandonment
But even in my nightmares
I had never imagined
Abandonment
While facing
Fighting
Cancer
If you believe
That someone
Unconditionally
Cares for you
Just get sick
See what they do

Grains of Sand

Memories
Fall through my fingers
Fine grains of sand
Eroded by time
By powerful waves of emotion
Birthed in my souls
Tumultuous ocean
I sift through them
Searching for meaning
Finding only more love

Stardust

The same stardust
Begat all of us
There is so much
Of the divine
In our humanity
With all our disagreements
And differences
I hope that we
Will someday come to see
We come from the same
Celestial source
There is no separation
Between a flower and a bee
We have the same color blood
All of us
Including you and me

Poetry

I've written
My heart out
Yet somehow
It's still here
Pumping blood
Through my hungry body
Reminding me of loss
With every beat

True North

Lost
In my own mind
Sometimes
I think I'll stay here
With my best friend
We're safe here
But eventually
I know
My internal compass
Will point me
To the true north
Of true love
I'll have no choice
I'll leave the safety
Of my solitude
And put my worn
But hopeful heart
Out naked on the line

Primeval

Passion erupts
In the darkest corners
Of my soul
Something birthed
At the beginning of time
Primeval
It owns me
Like dark owns the stars
Letting me know
In no uncertain terms
That I have never been in charge

Enough

And I am still so happy
That we live on the same planet
That you exist
I can shower you with love
From a distance
While still holding
An abundance in my heart

I have enough
I am enough
Without you

Near Miss

Everything I never said
And some things I did
I write
Sometimes even I can't believe
The sadness
Of my feelings
How much
I have missed
A near miss
Nearly loved me
Nearly mine
Nearly made it
At this point
I can say
That I am nearly
Over it

Don't Say

Someday
Don't say I passed away
Say that I died
Say that until I died
I truly lived
There is no passing
Demurely
To other side
For a woman like me
I'm going to die
When I'm done living
I'm going to live
Until I die

I started writing as a kind of therapy, to get myself out of a deep hole. I would suggest it to anyone, there is nothing more transformative than creative expression. The scars, both physical and emotional are fading with each word I type.

Thank you Sarah Melland for casually suggesting I publish after having such success with it yourself.

Thank you, mom and dad for taking care of me at my most vulnerable. I'll try not to grow anymore tumors.

All of this is true, all of it is false. I write what I'm feeling in the moment and every moment is different. My writing is often sad because I have to put my shadow side somewhere. I am, however, a reasonably happy person who happens to have been through some relatively bad times. Whatever you're going through, you can get through it. I promise, just hang on!!!

@poet_on_fire

Made in the USA
Middletown, DE
04 April 2018